Coloring book for adults and kids beautiful necklace

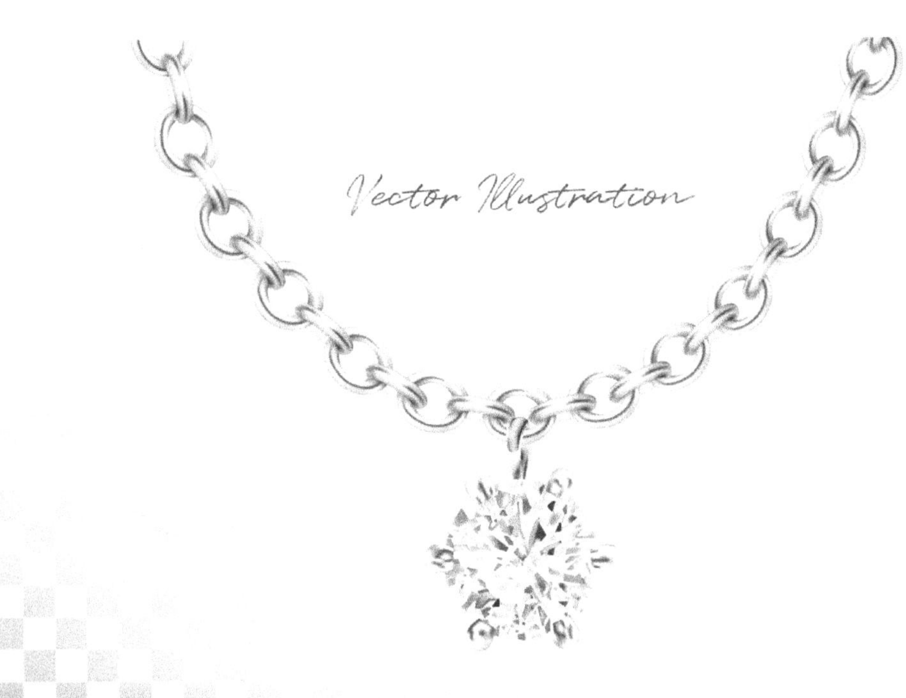

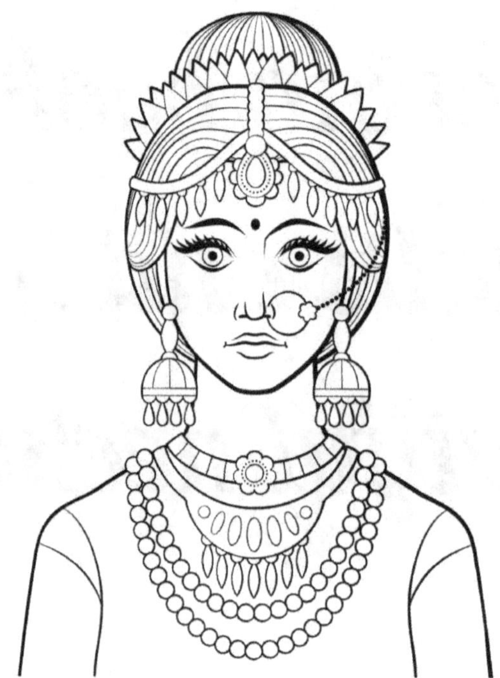

This book is belongs to

____

____

____

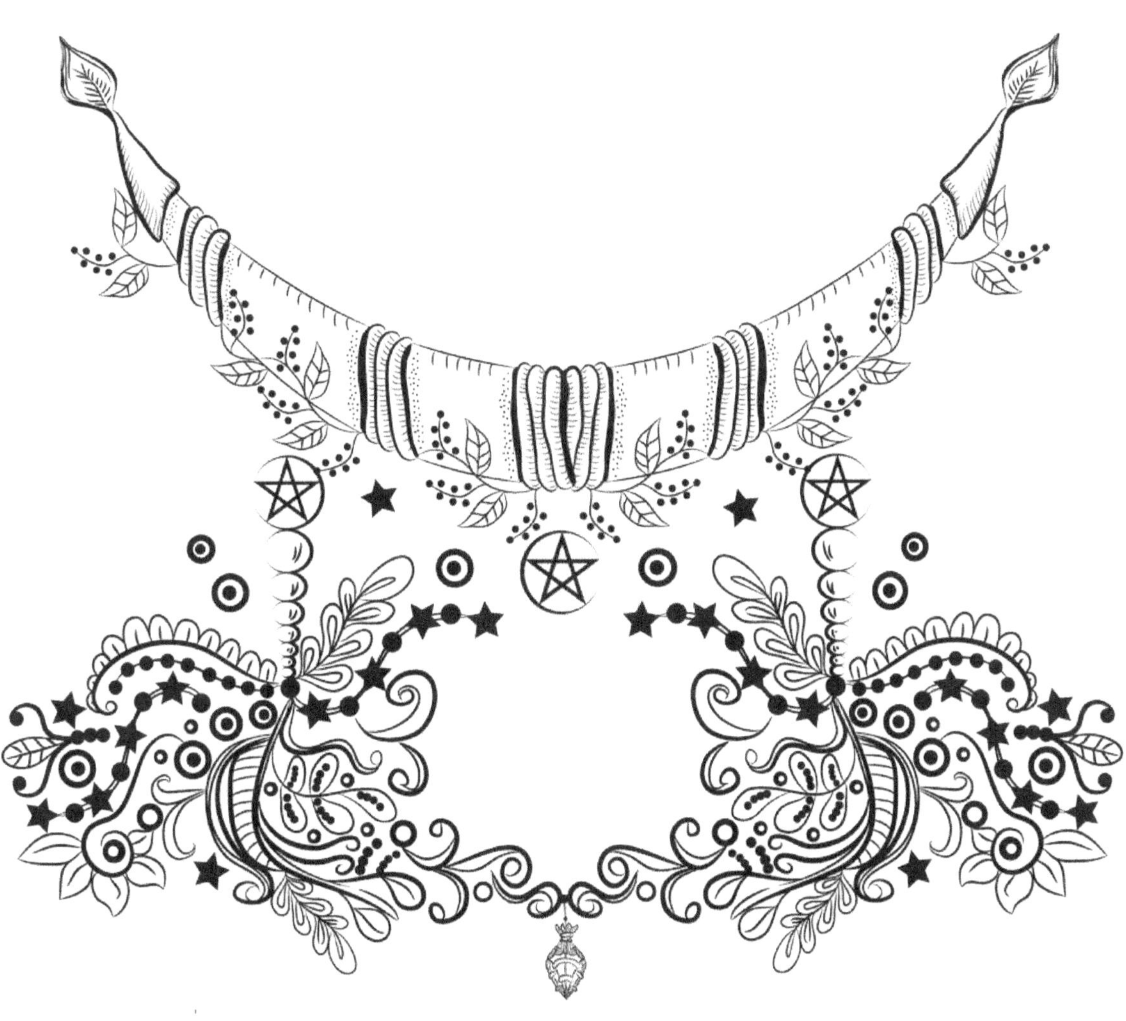

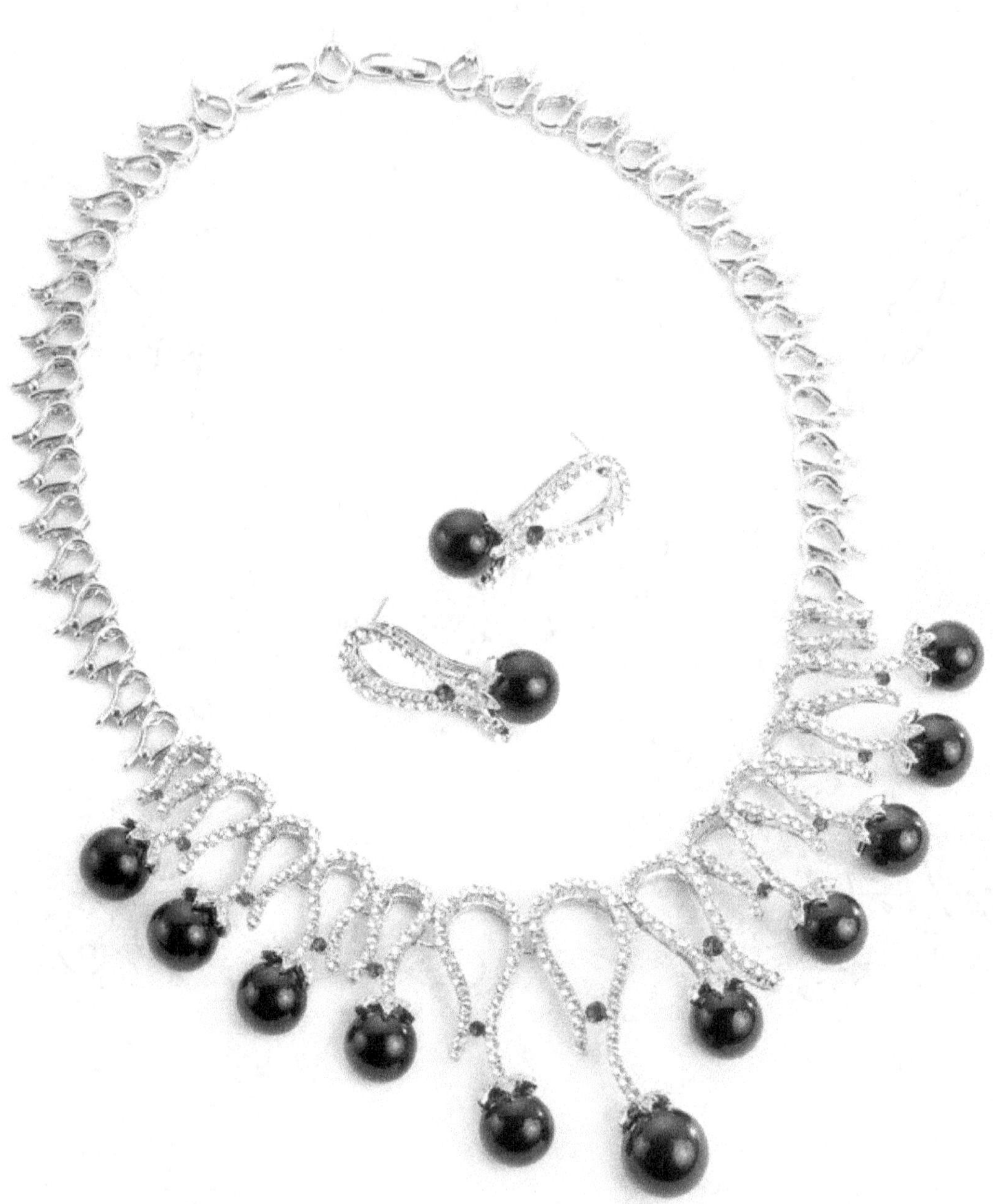

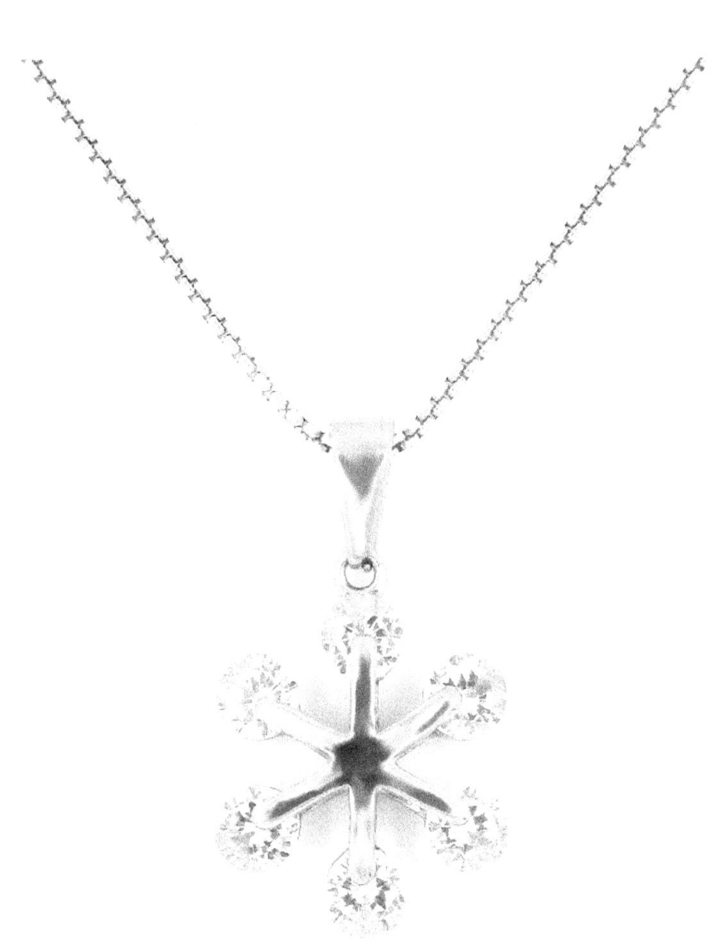

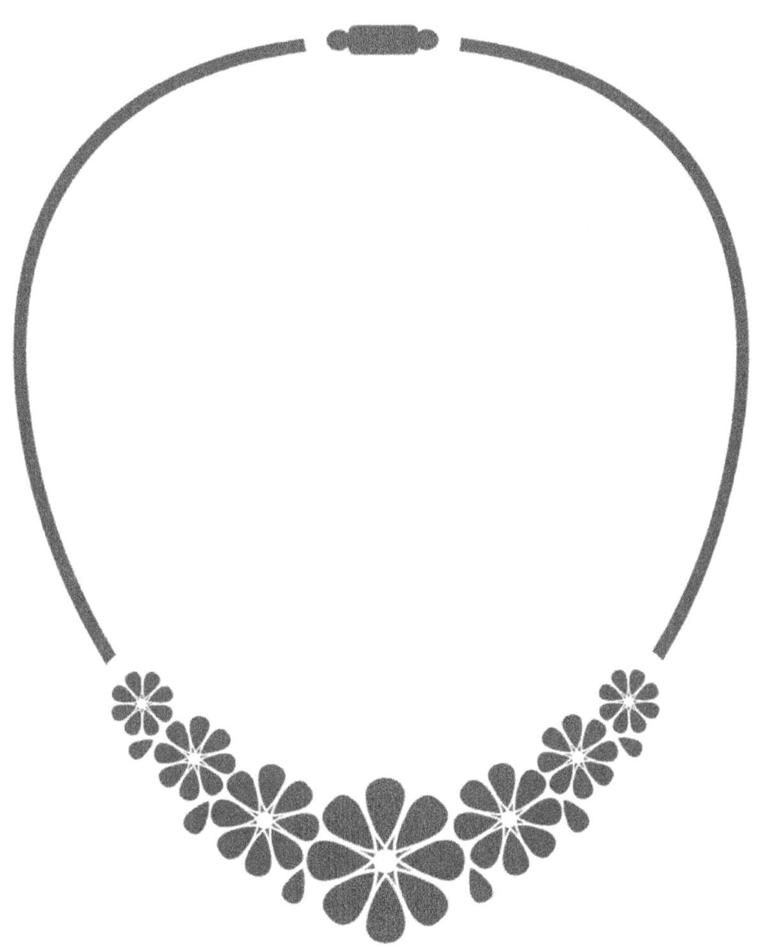

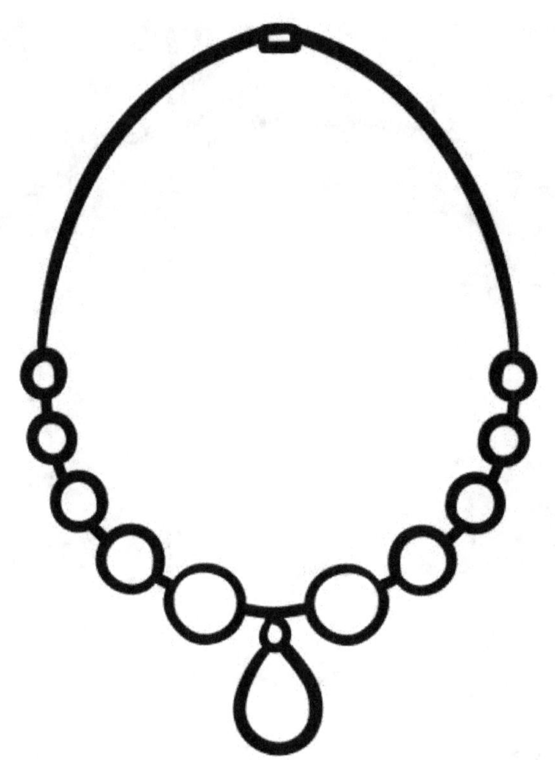

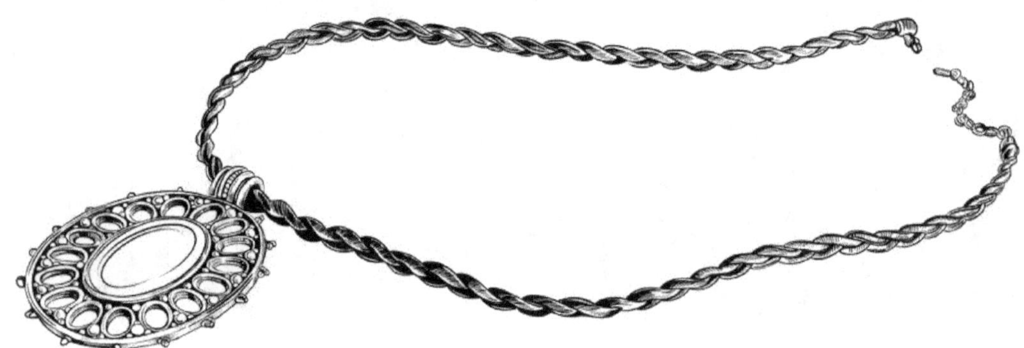

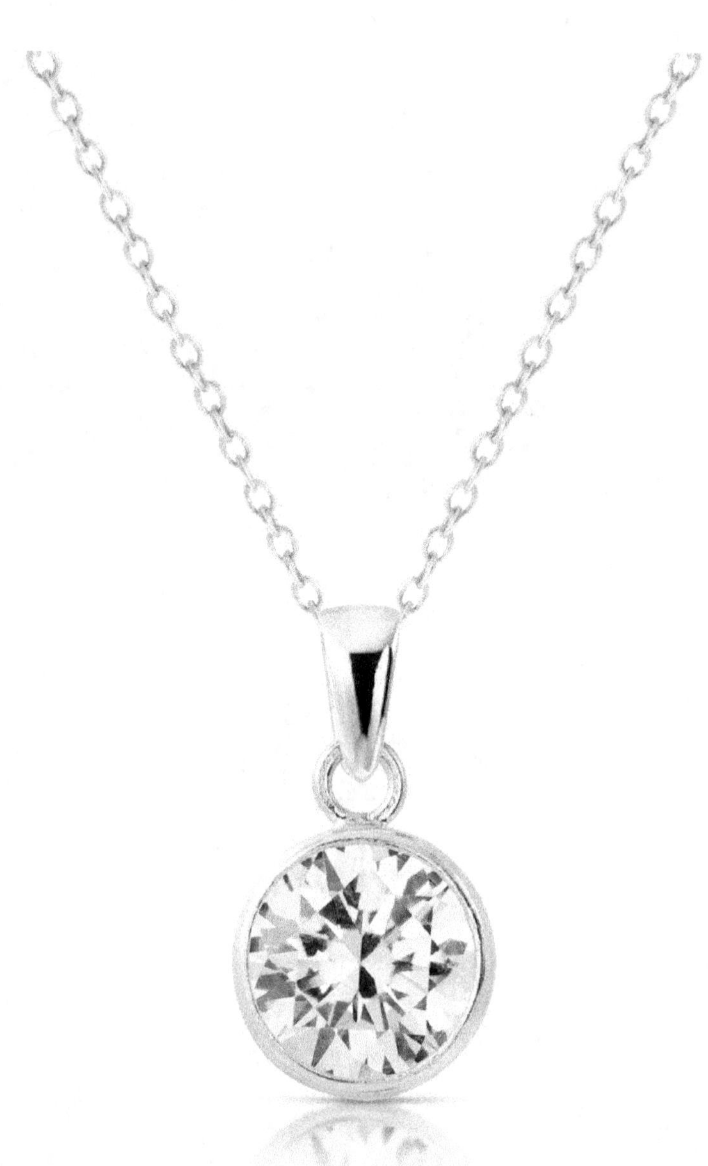

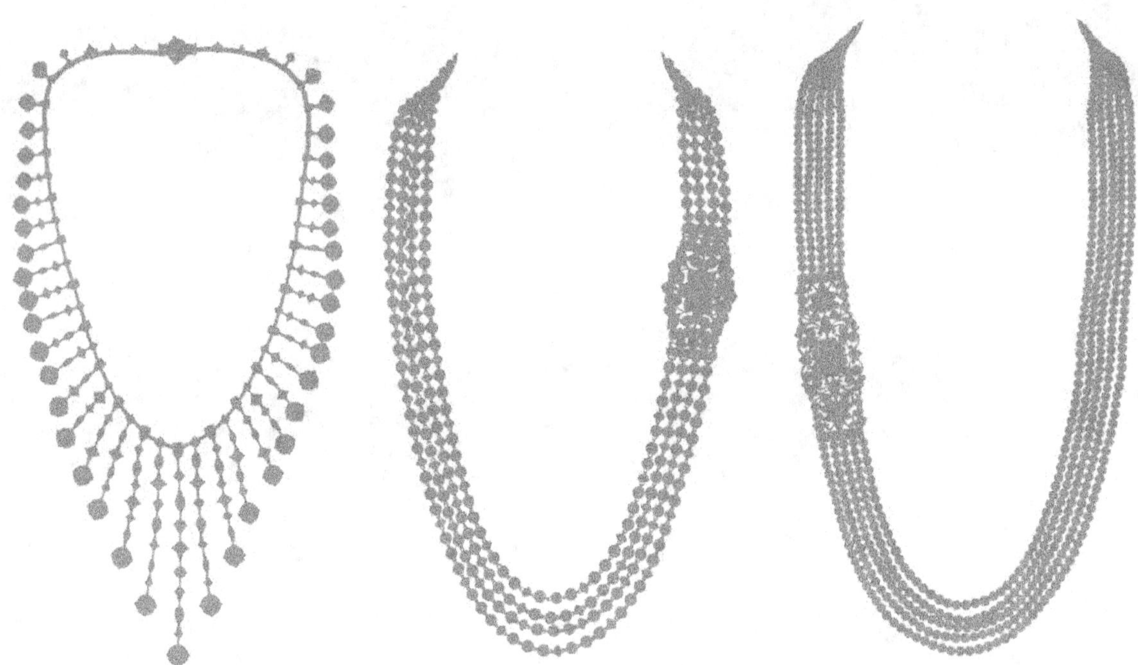

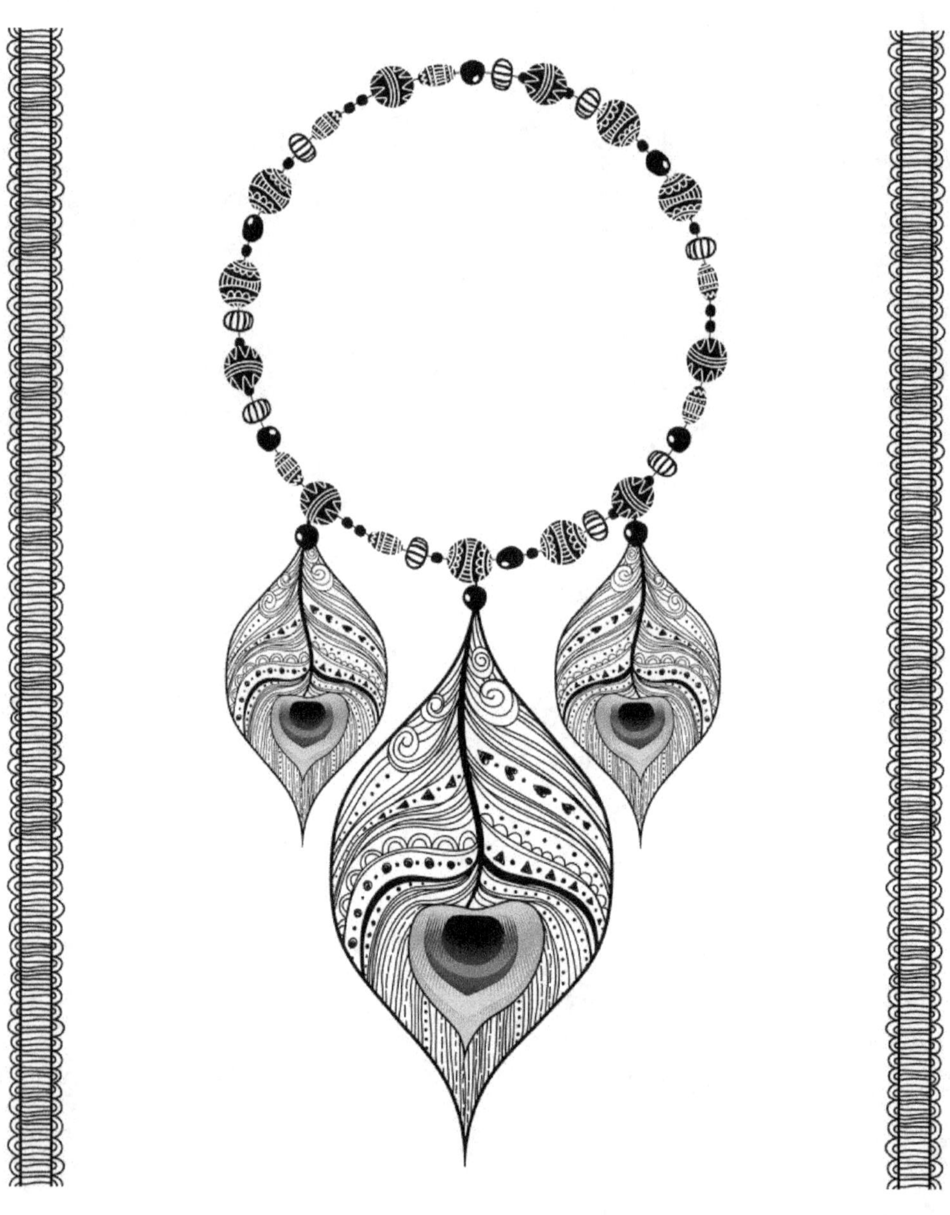

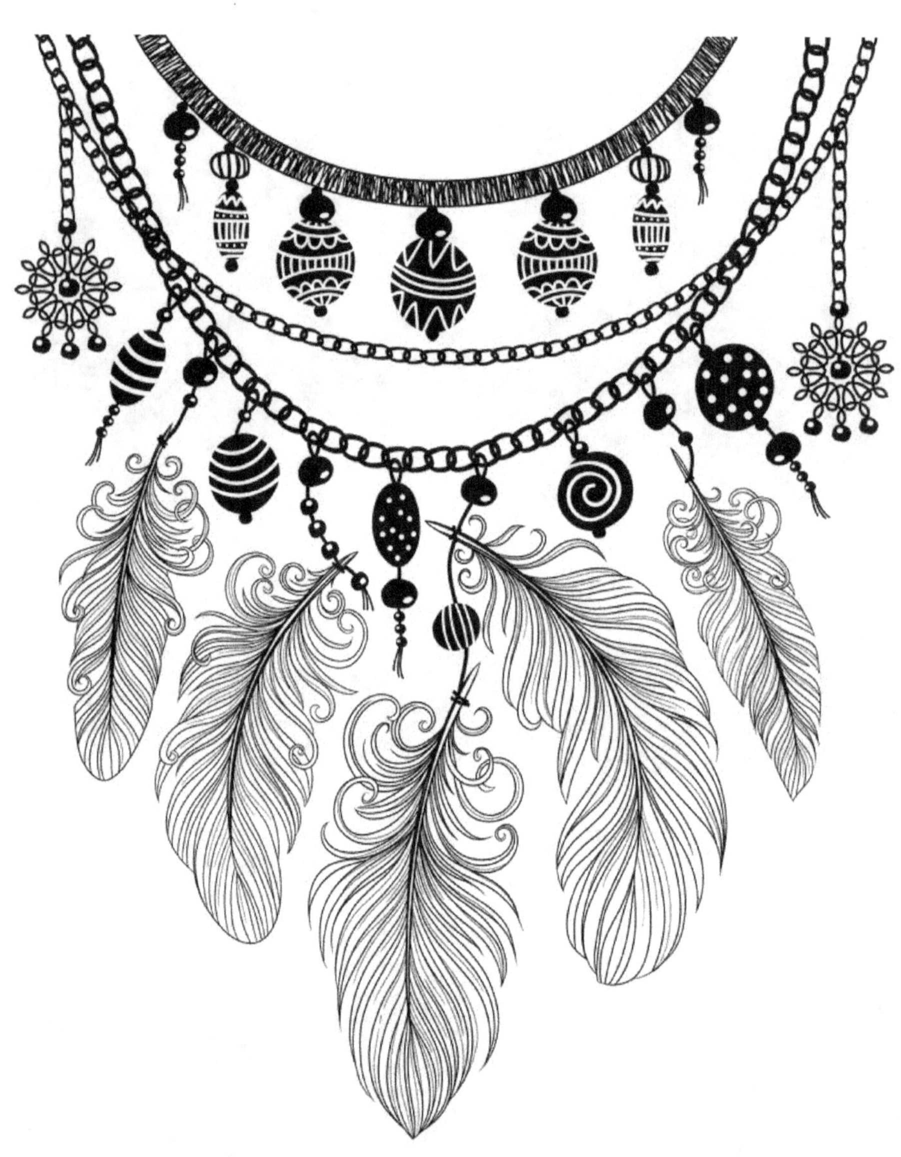

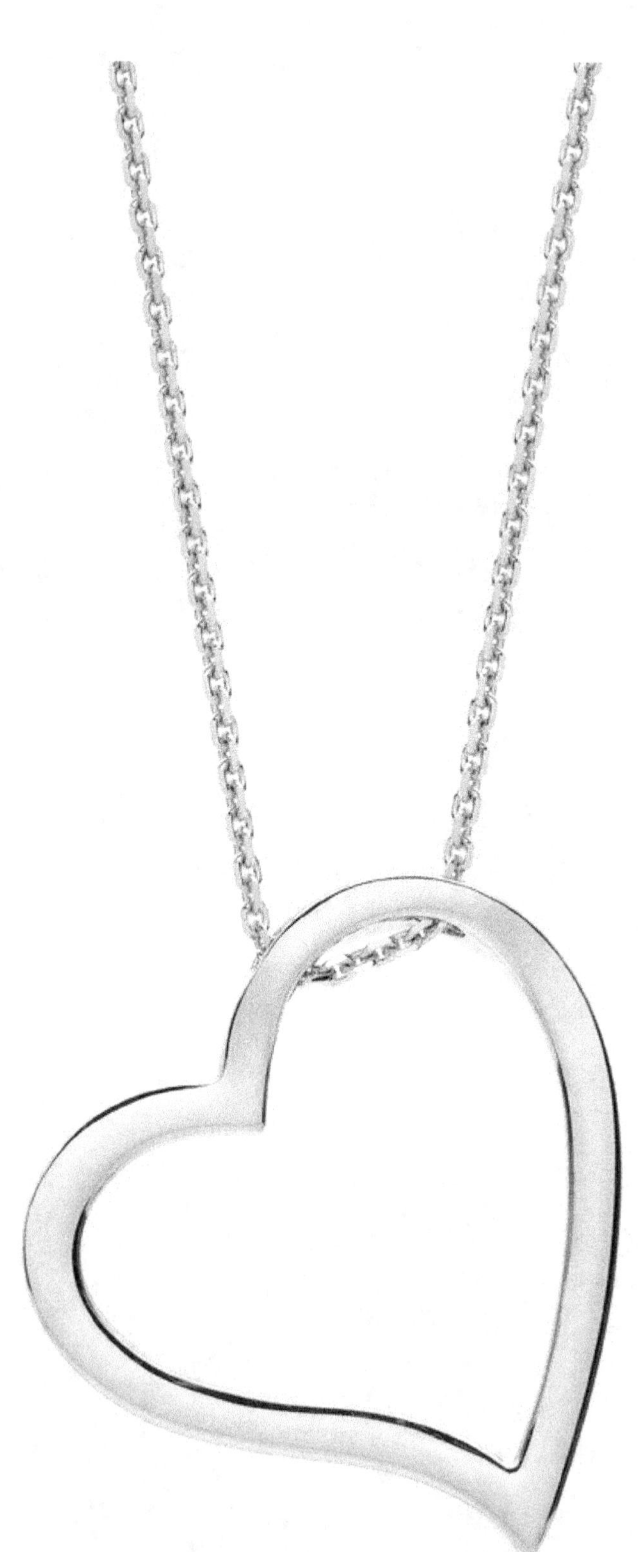

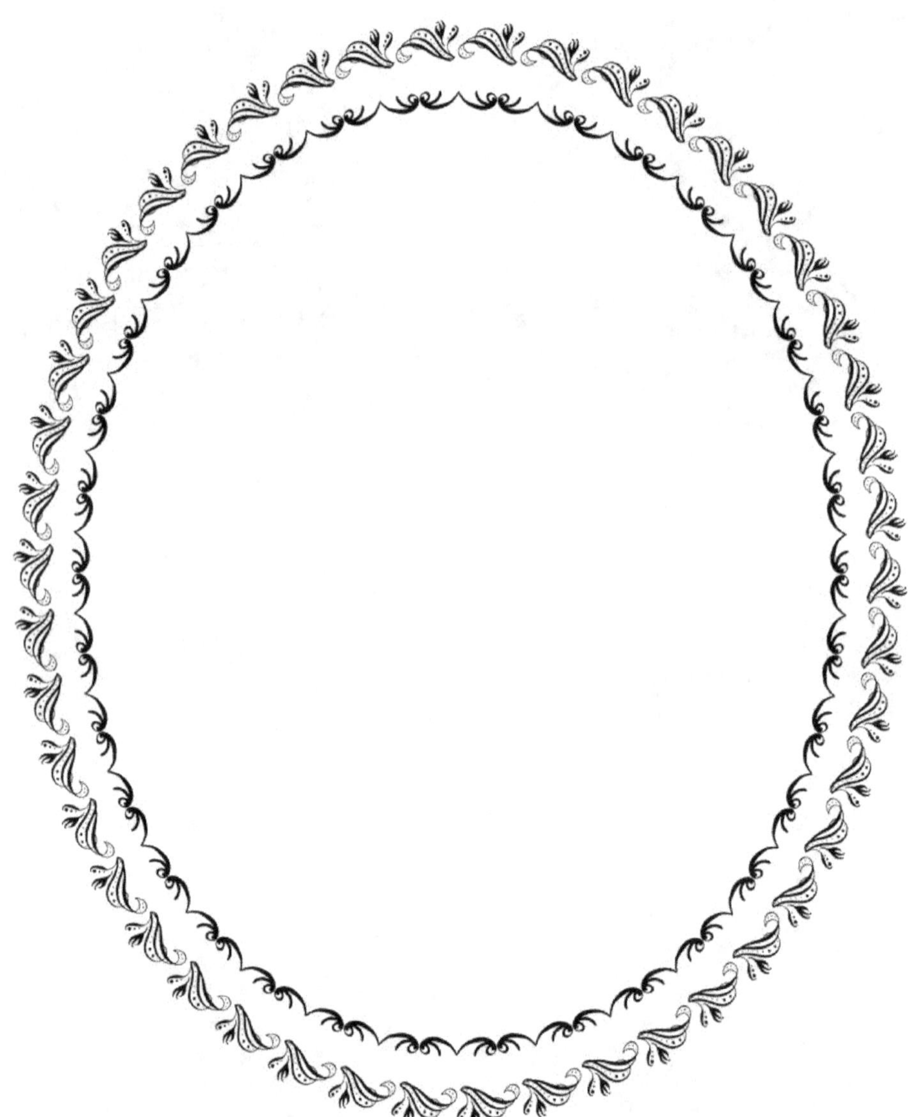

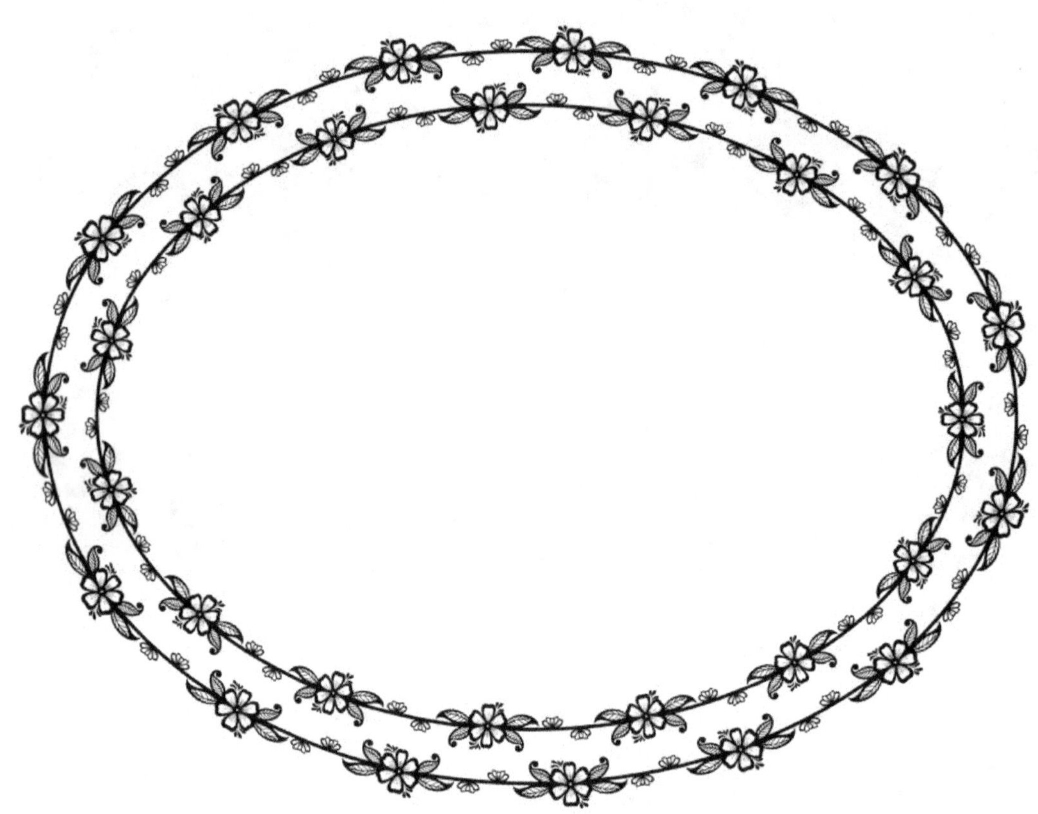

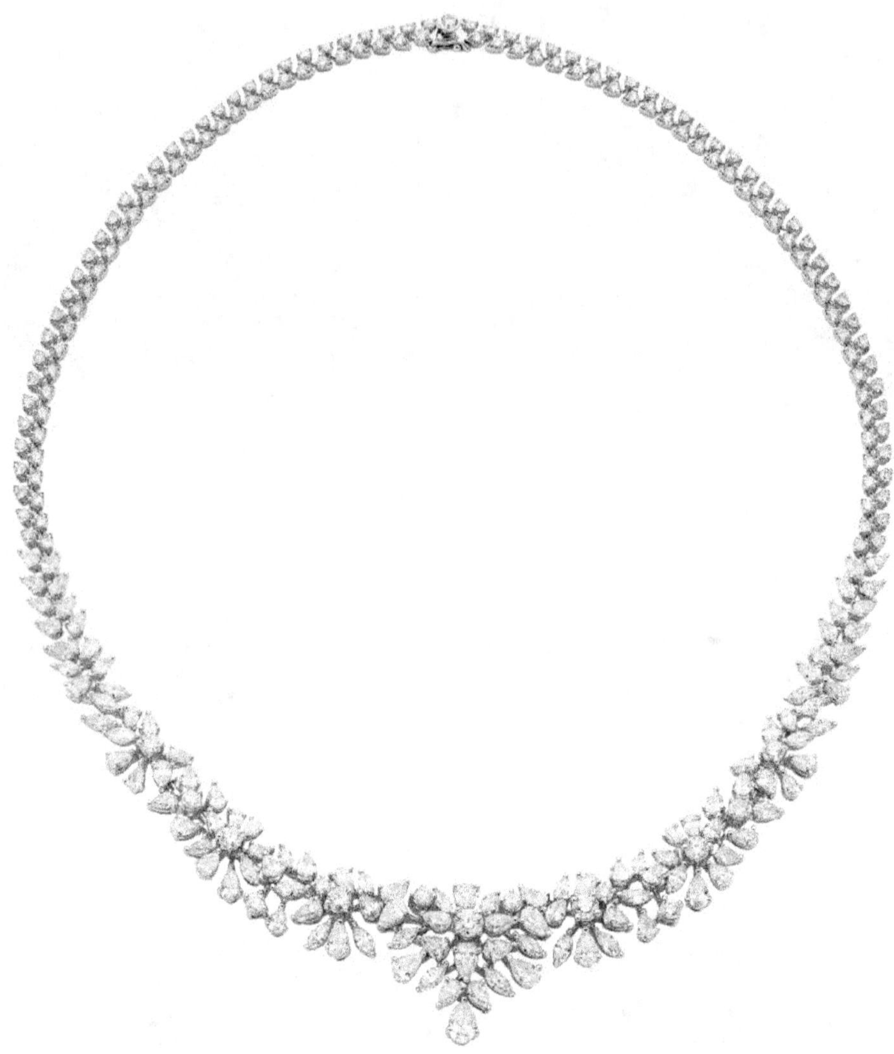

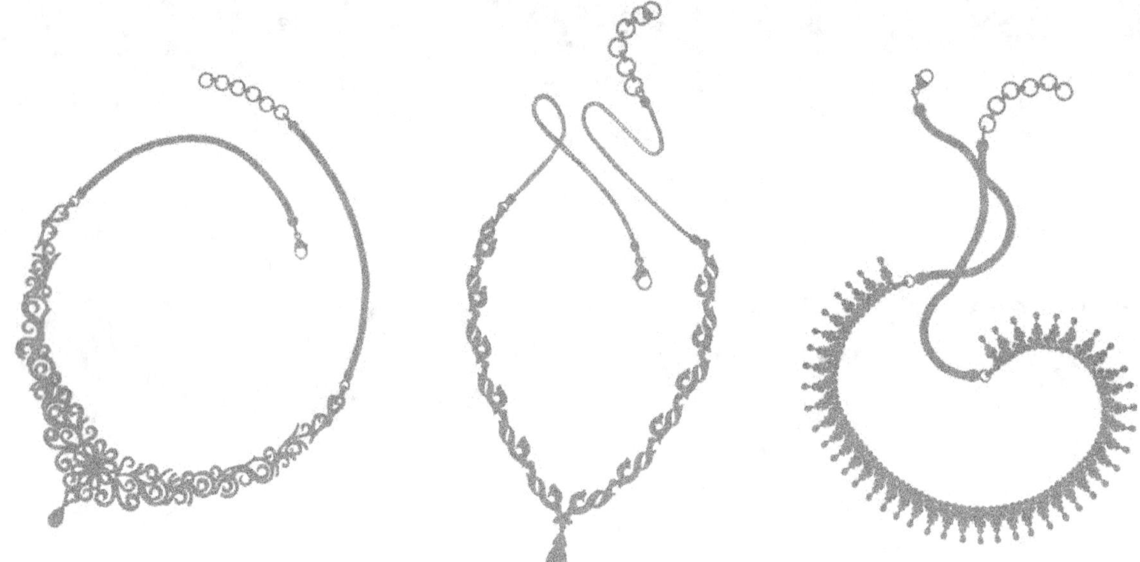

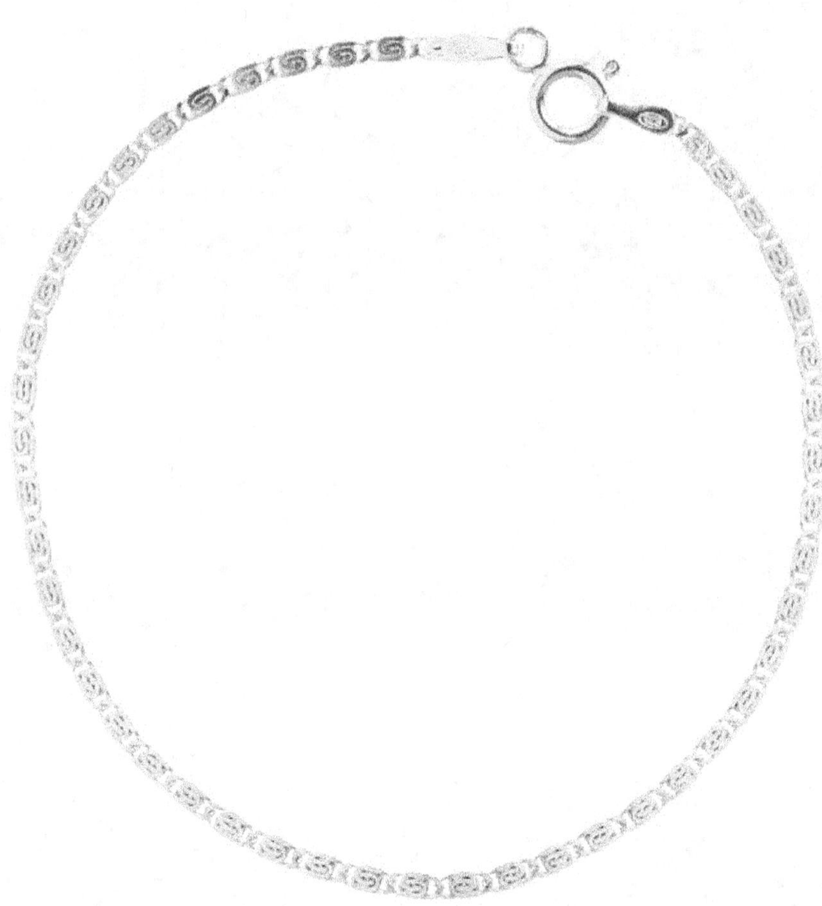

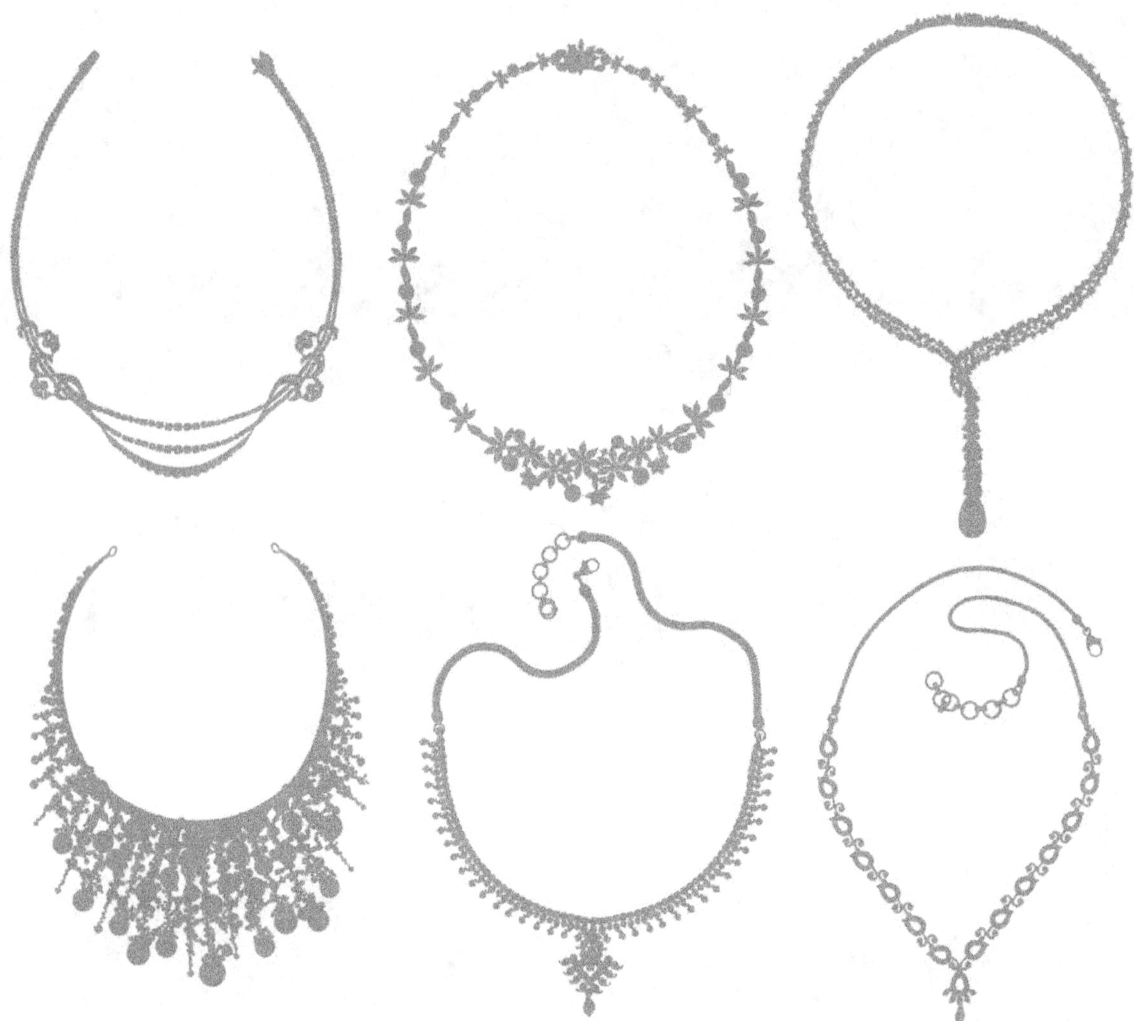

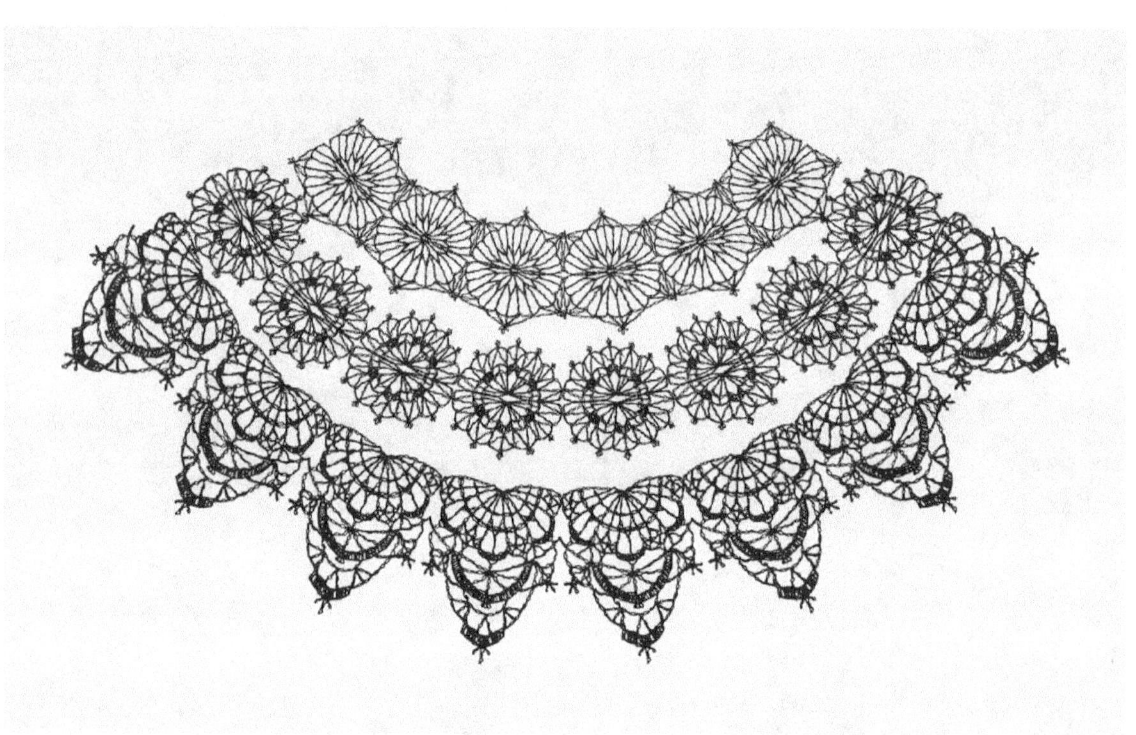

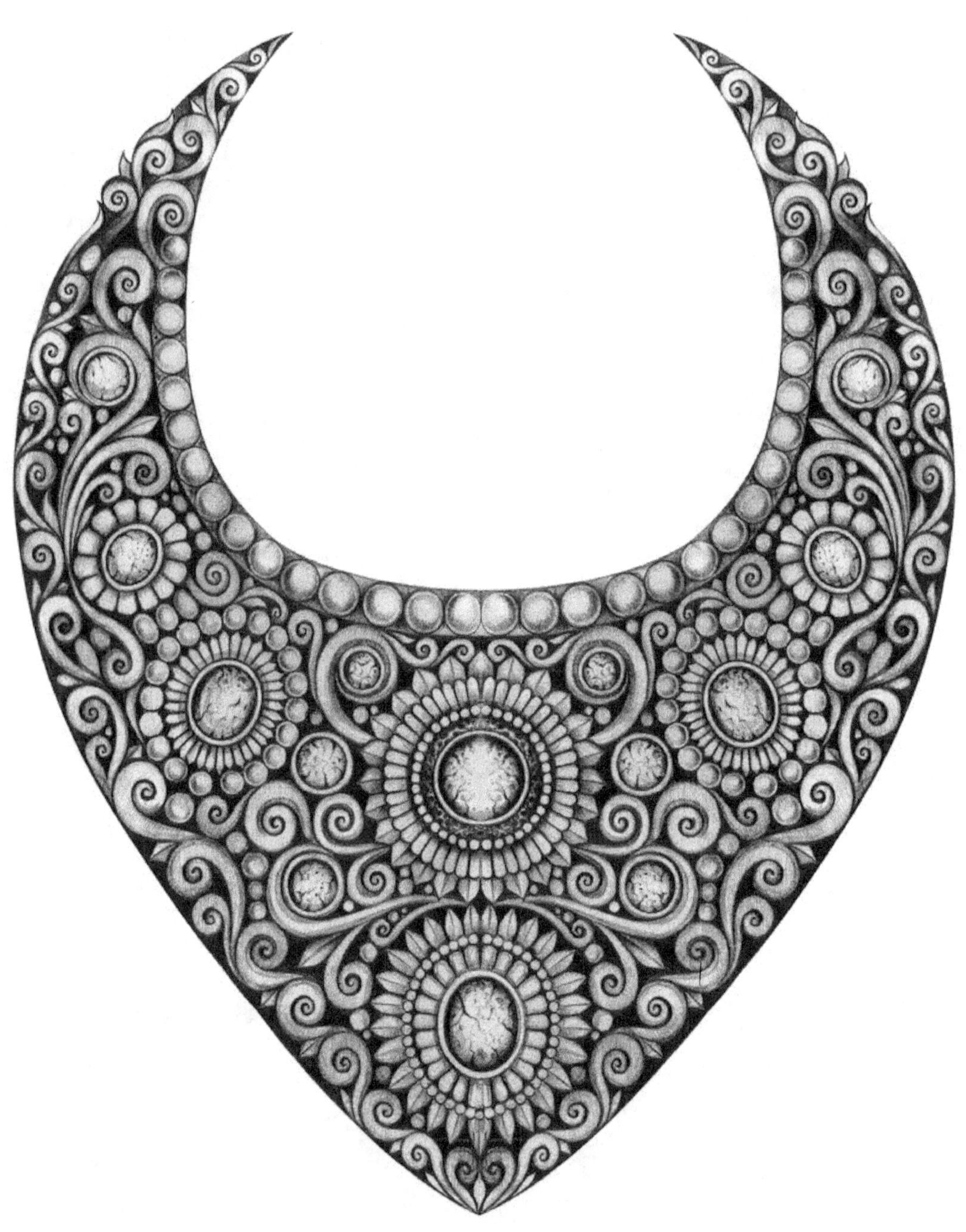

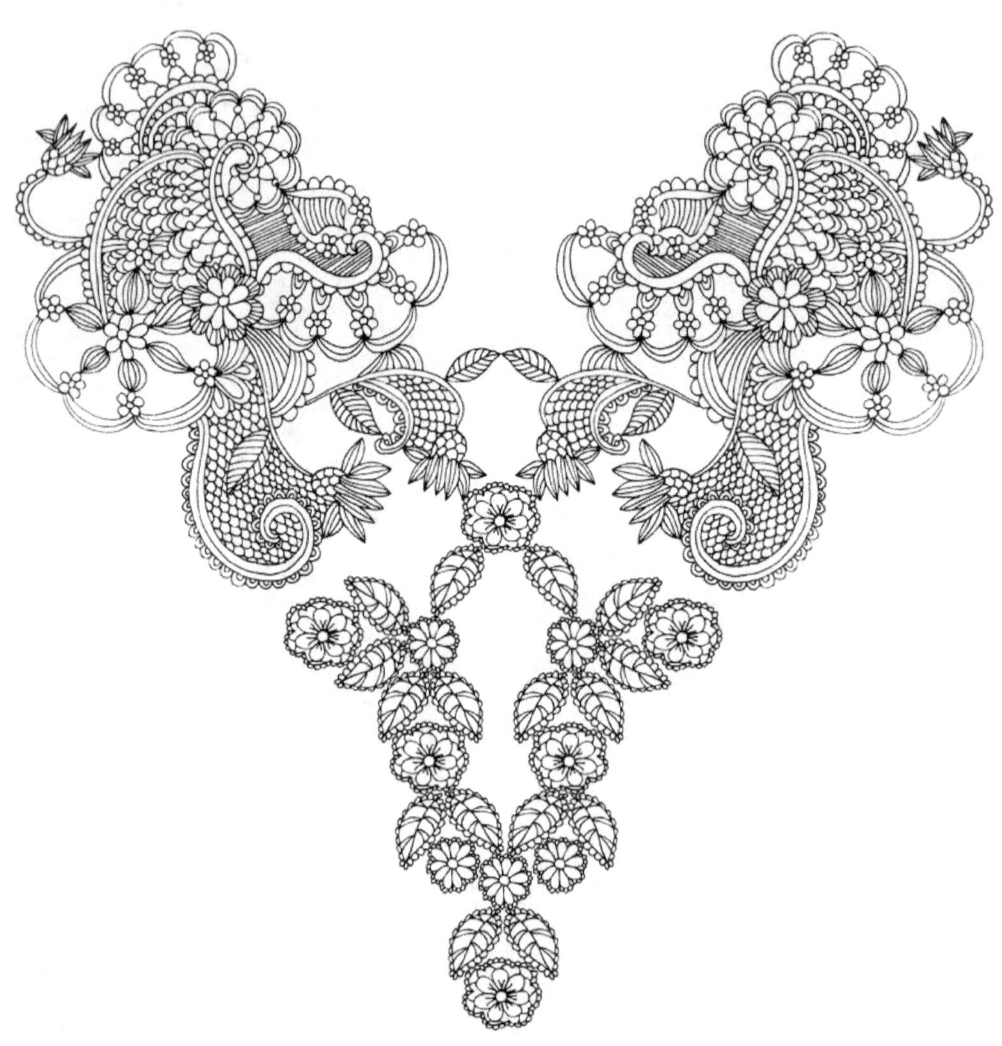

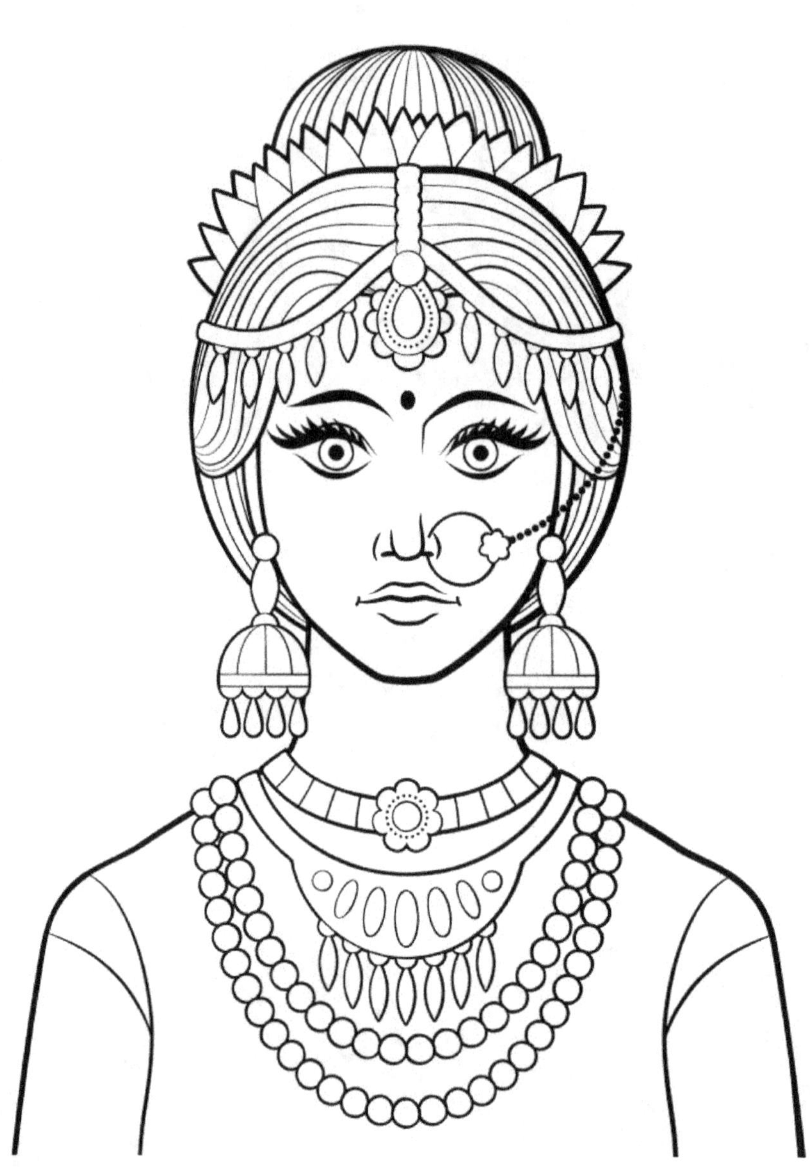

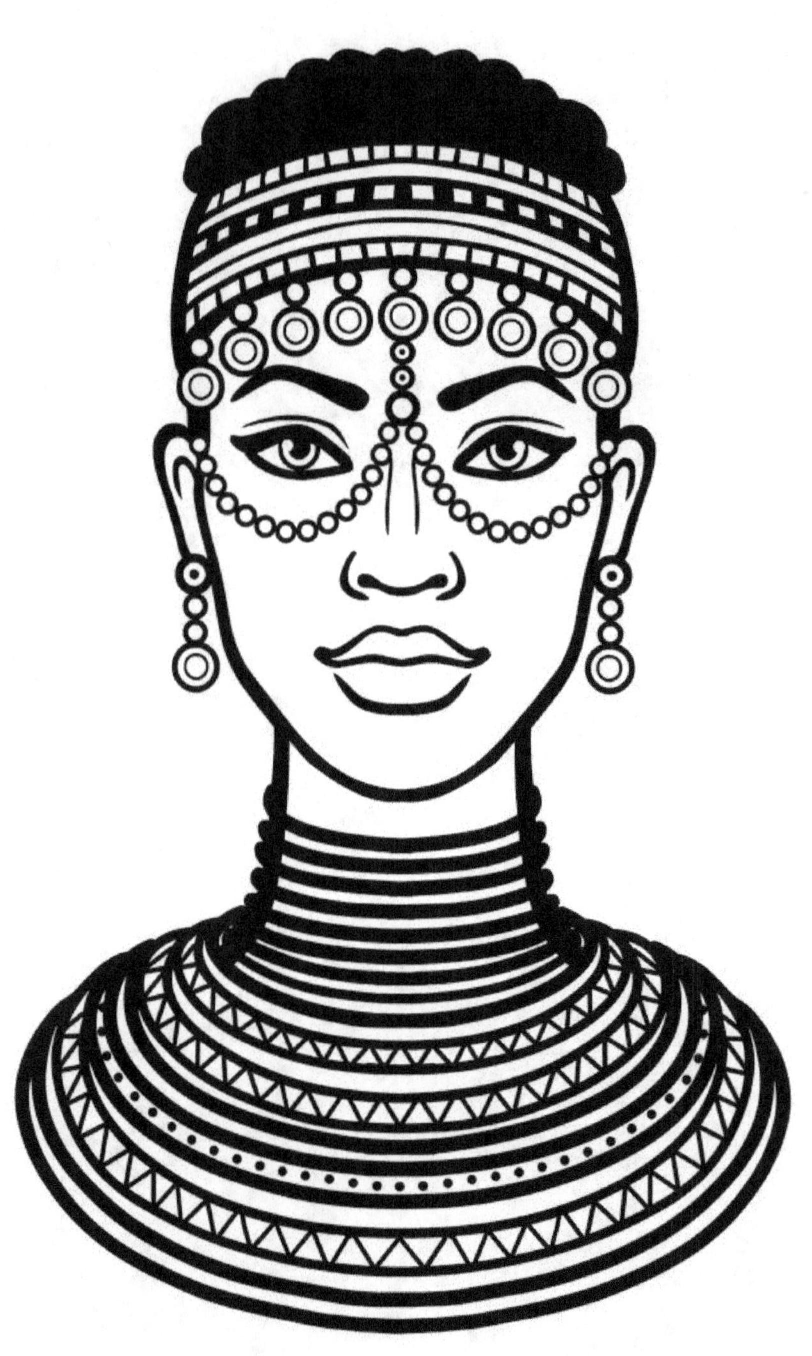

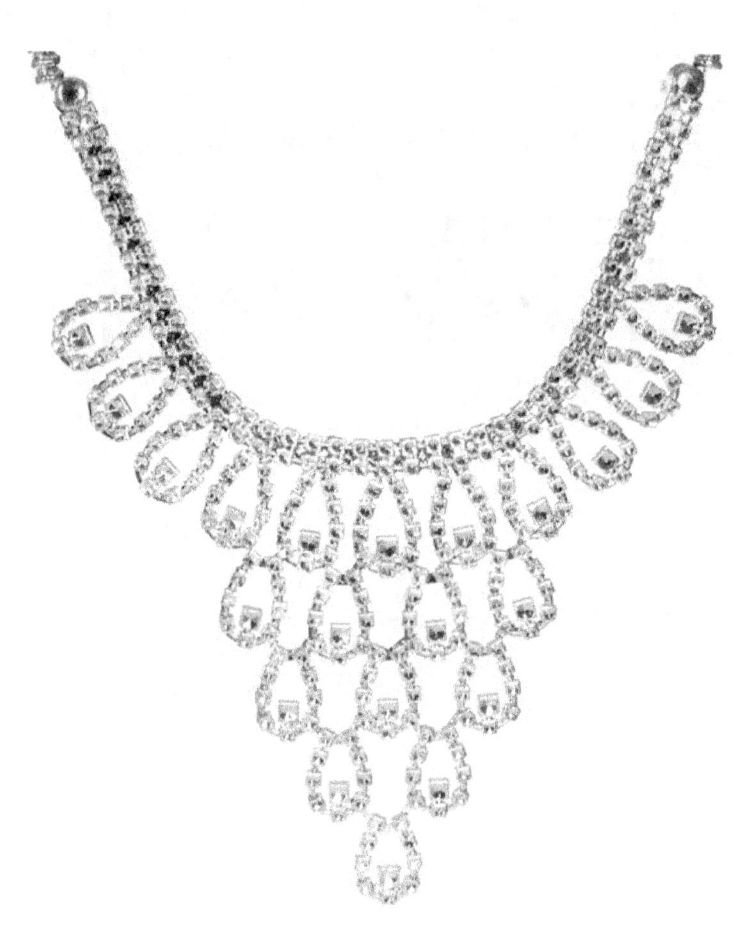

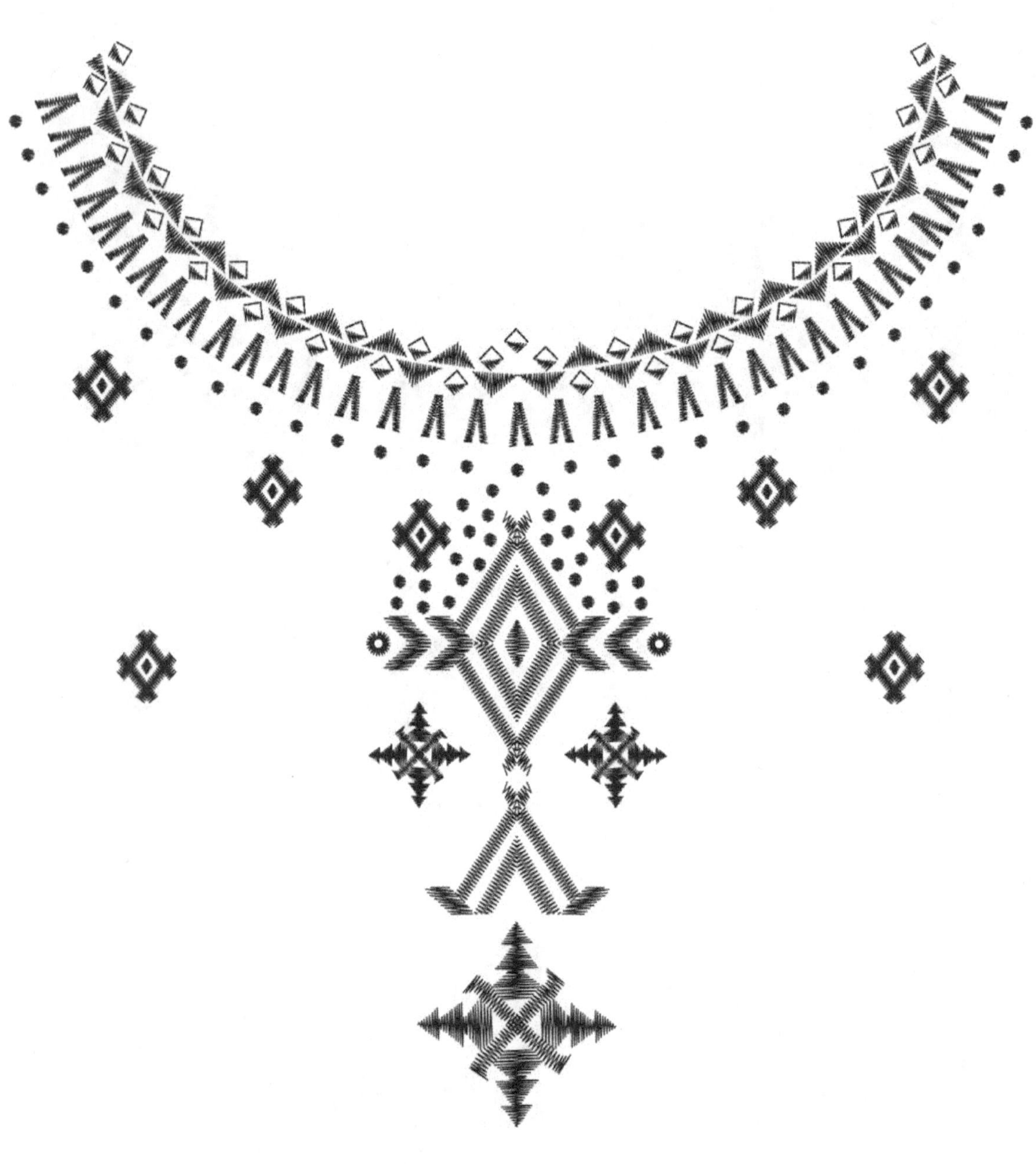

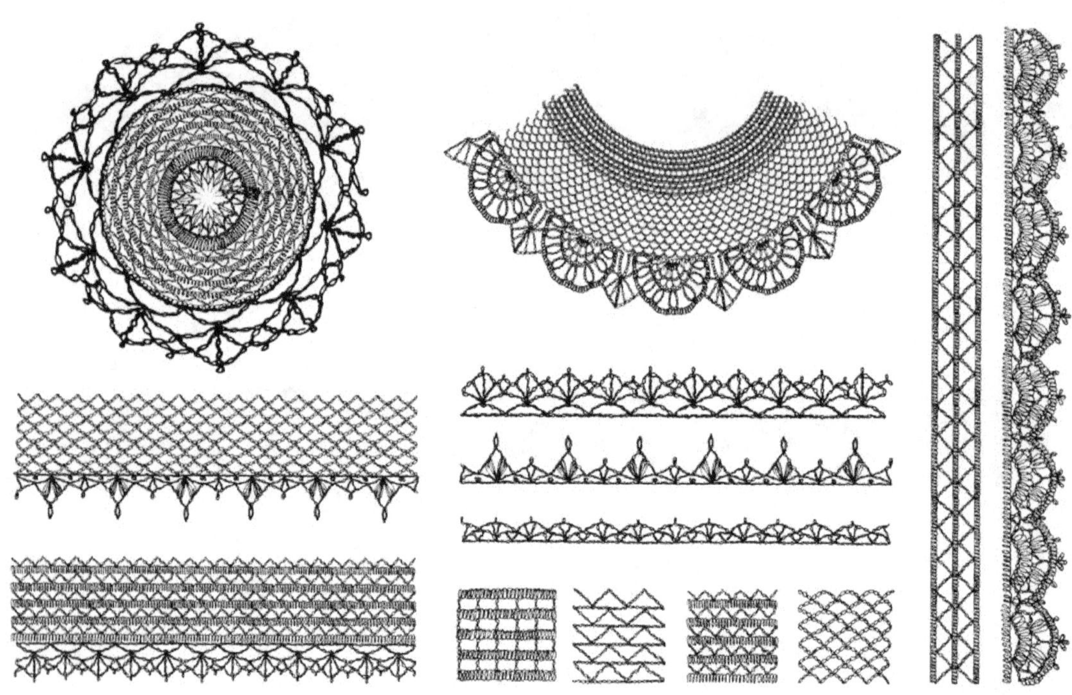

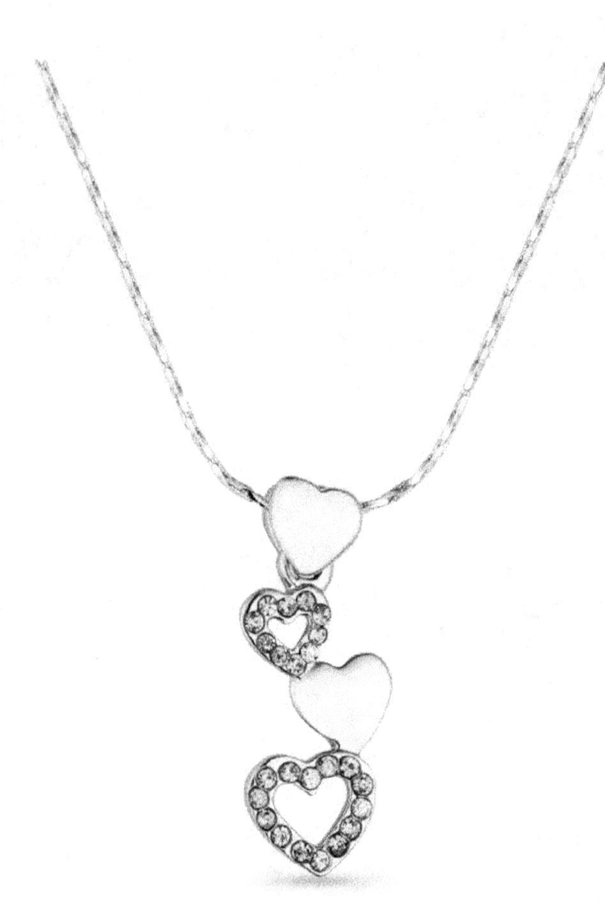

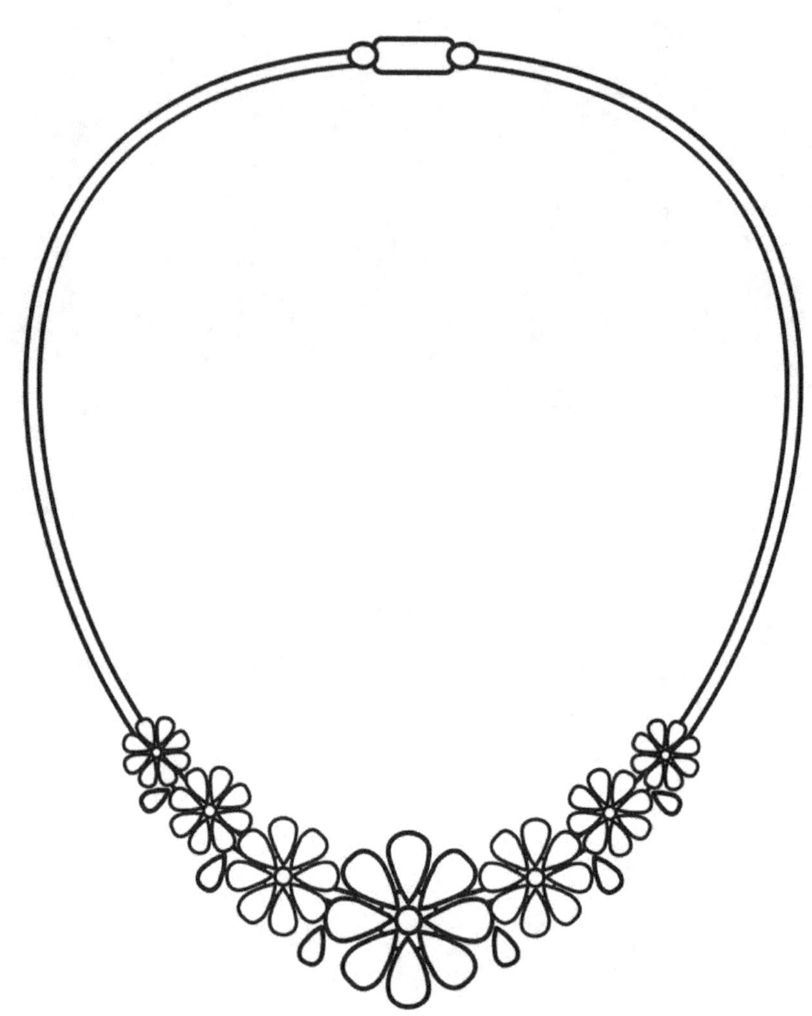

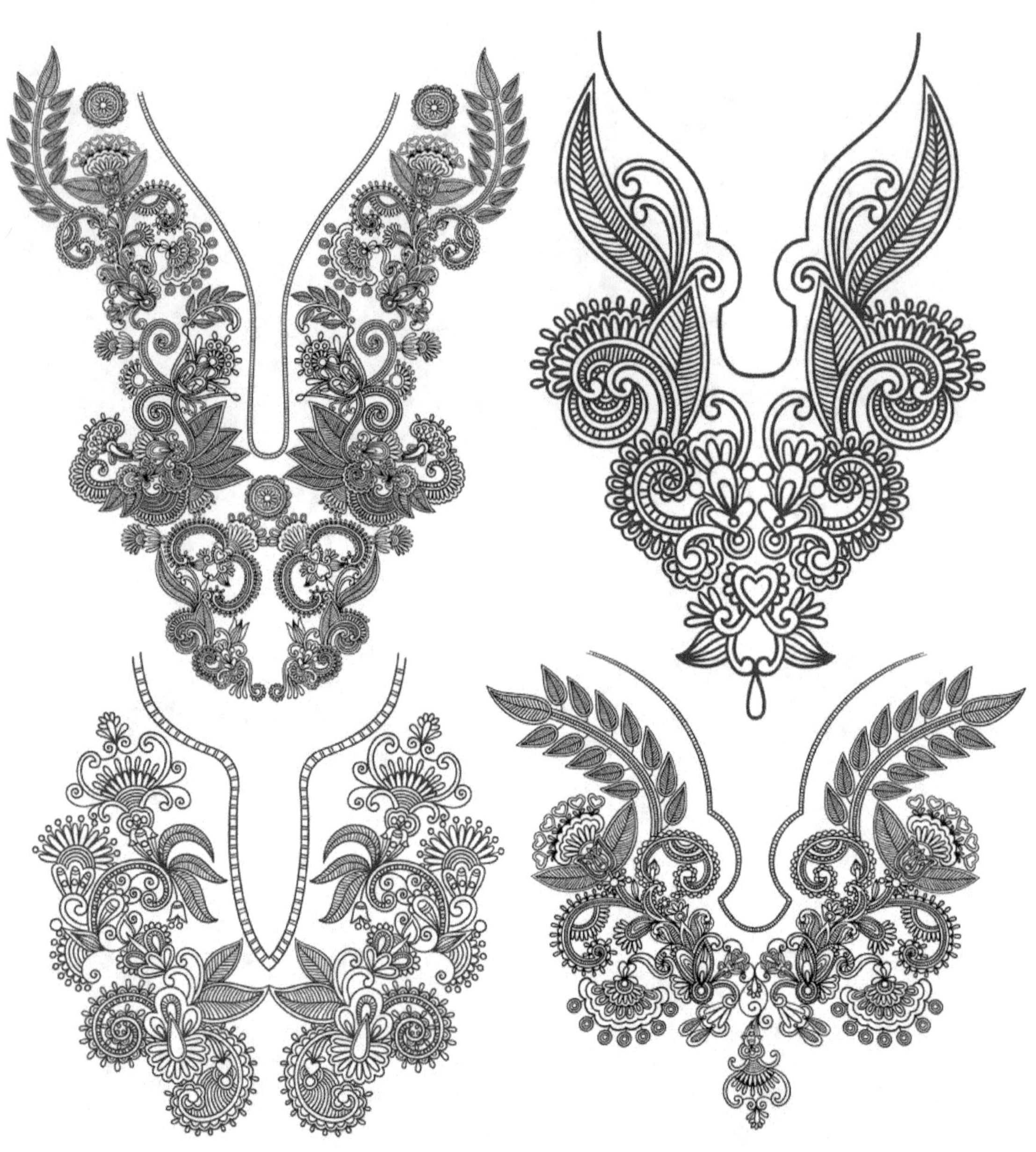

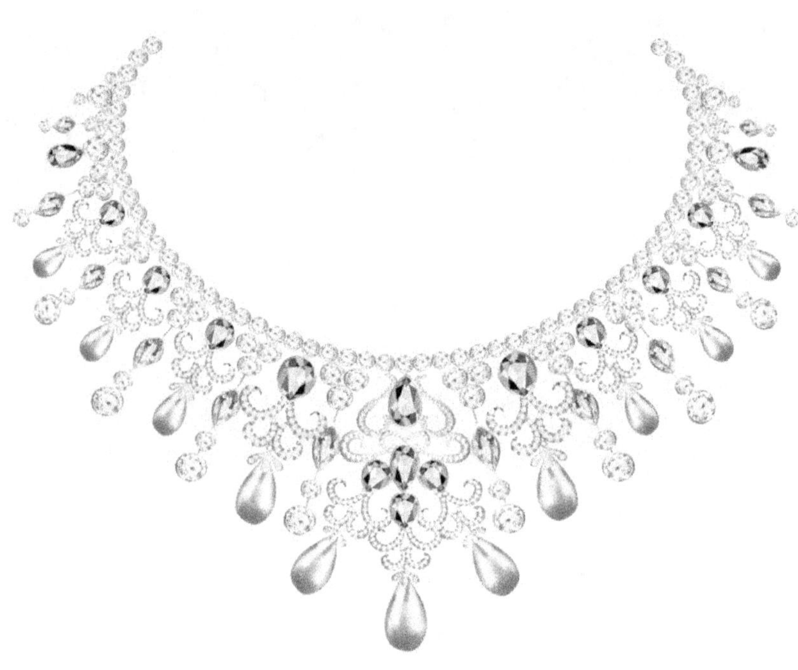

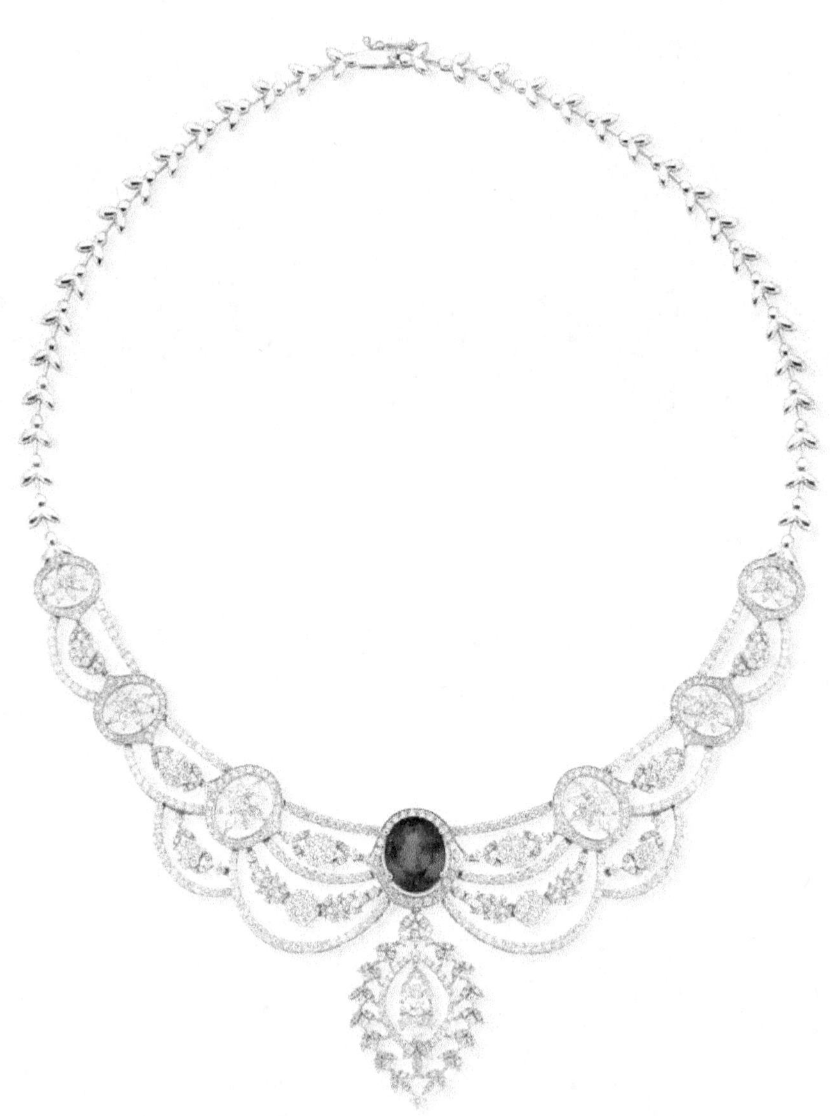

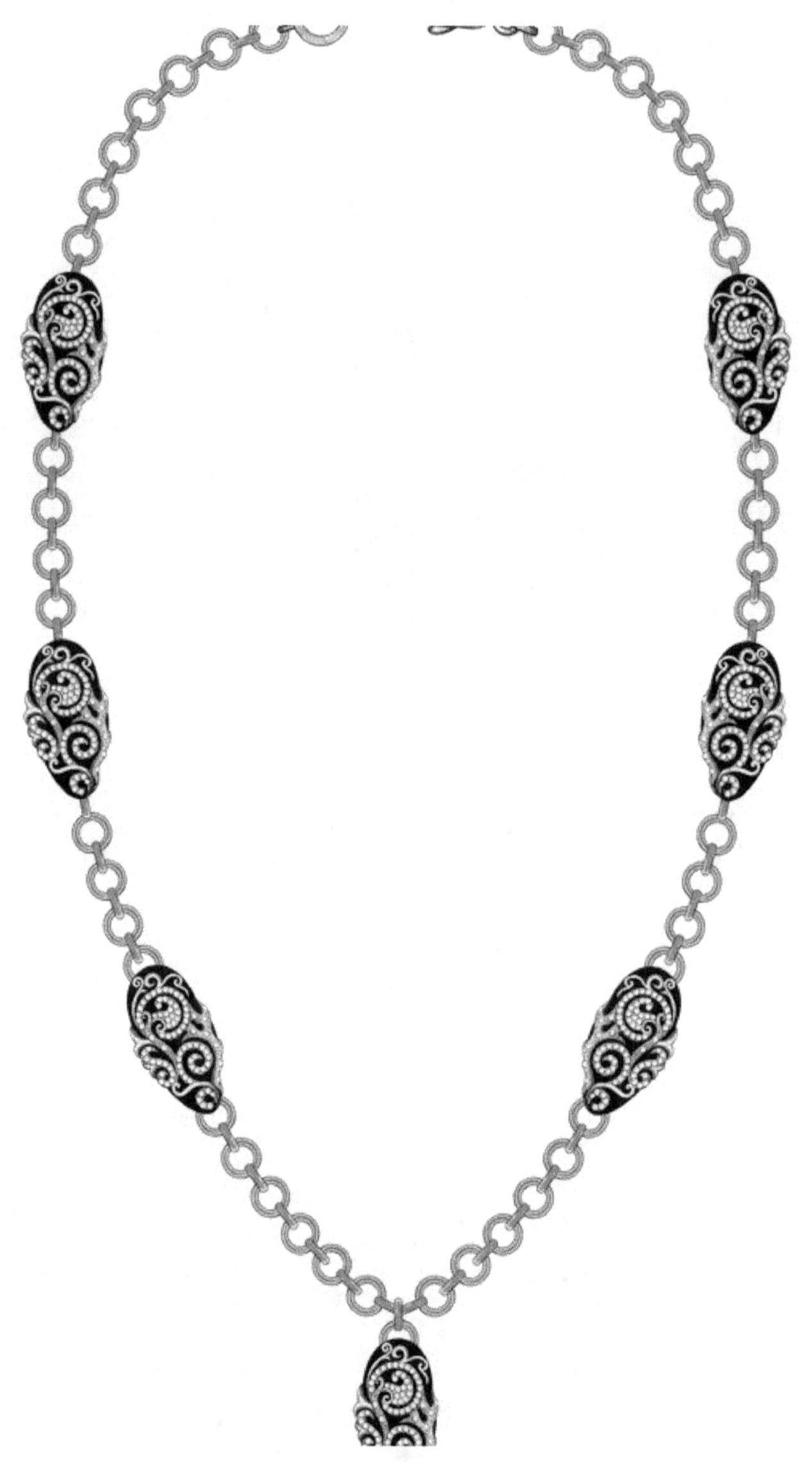

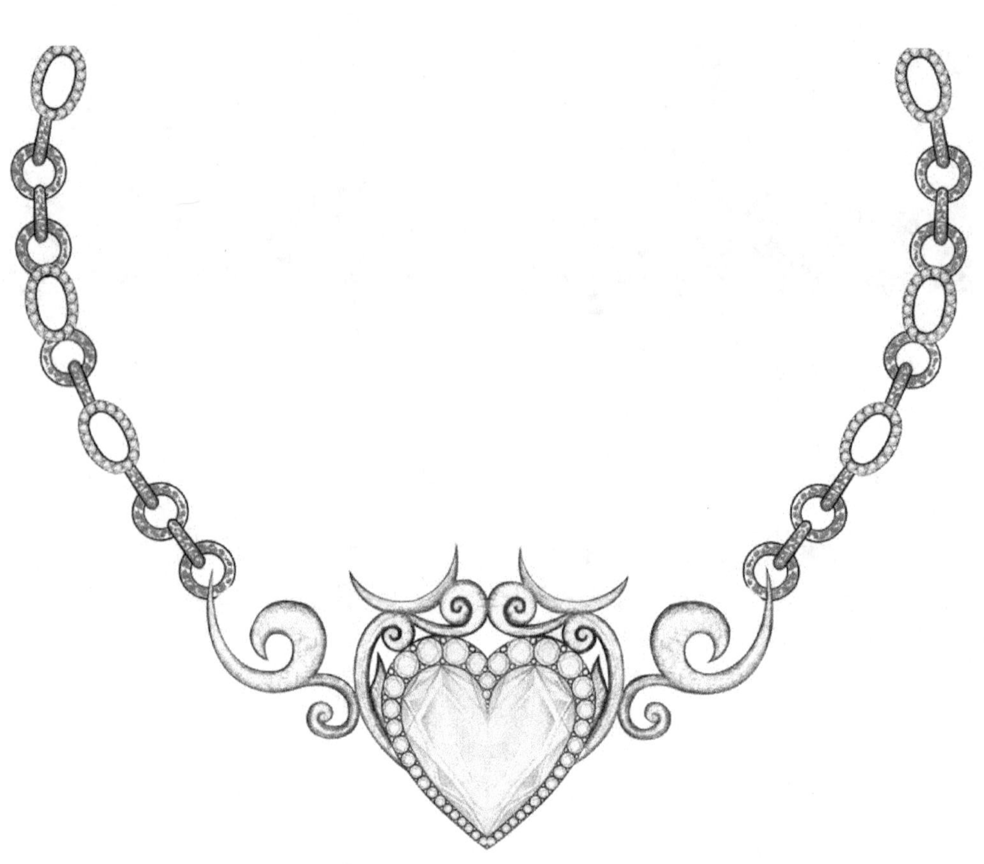

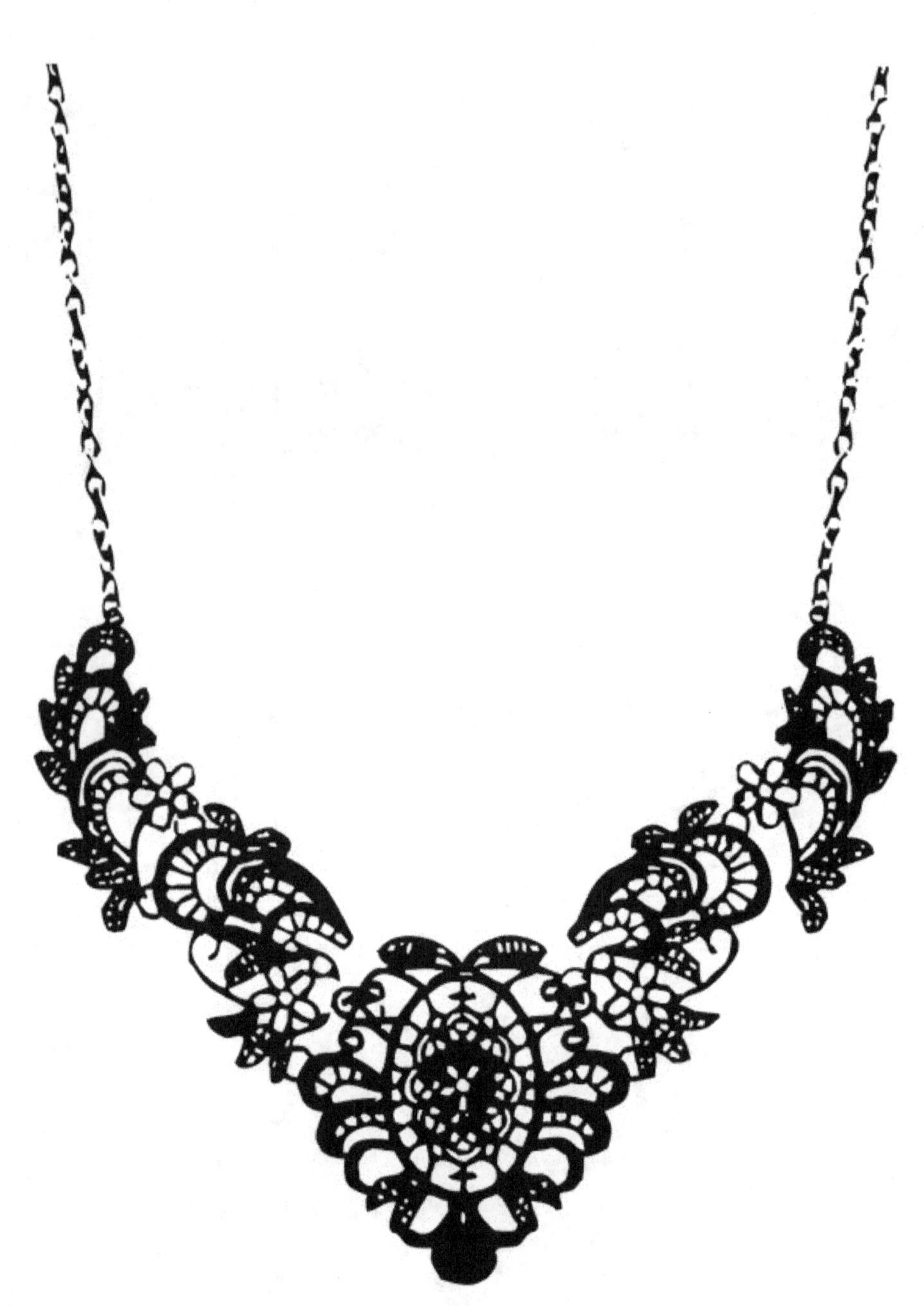

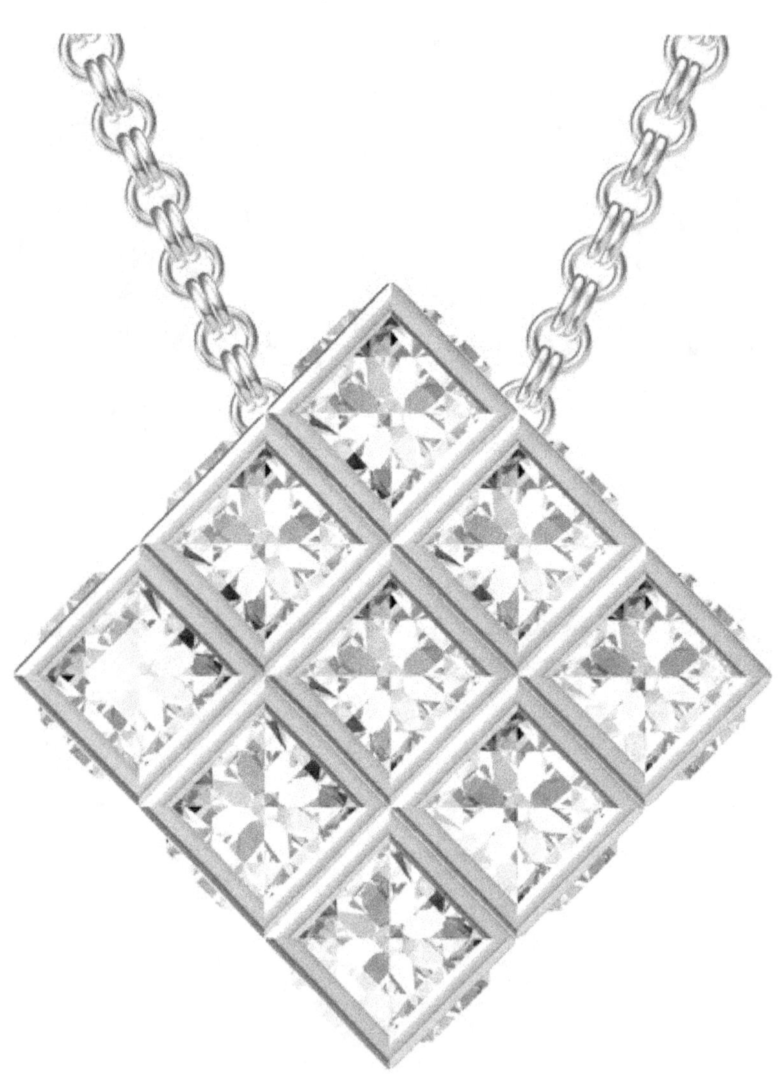

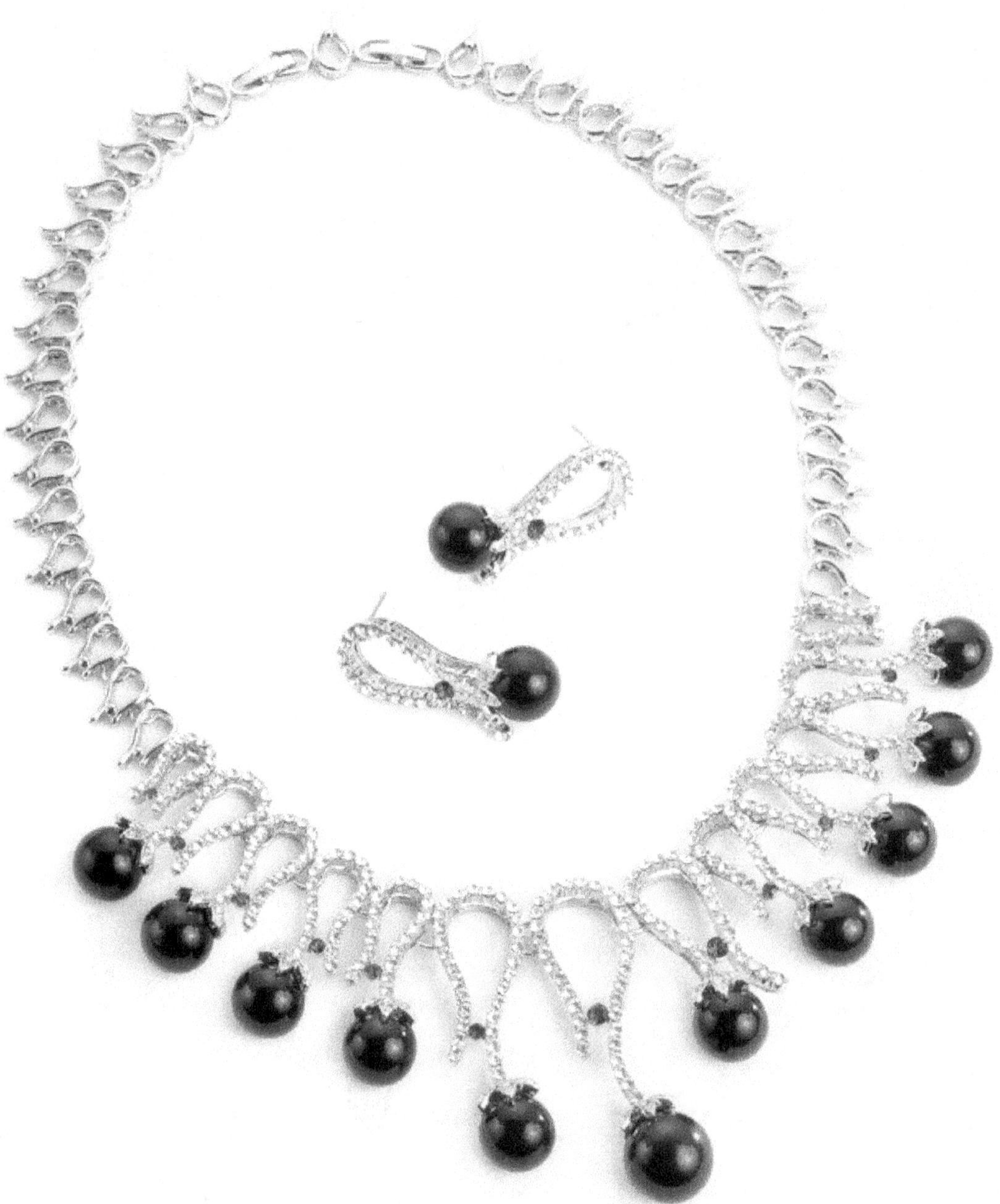